# Abingdon's Easter Drama and Program Collection

 Abingdon Press

# Contents

# MAUNDY THURSDAY LAST SUPPER REENACTMENT

## Arranged by Clark C. Christian

*The company is divided among twelve tables. Sufficient bread and juice should be ready on a center table for distribution at the appropriate time.*

**WELCOME AND INVITATION:** Welcome to this service. We will be enacting tonight the events of Jesus' last night with his disciples. We begin near Jerusalem, with each of us taking our part in the drama. Upon your table you will find scripts, parts of which are marked with your table number. Please join in reading those parts marked with your table number and of course all parts marked "ALL." Let us join now in this solemn act of remembrance, recognizing who we are in the presence of Jesus Christ our Lord.

**UNISON PRAYER:** O Christ, in your presence we discover who we are. We are not always faithful. We do not always fulfill the potential you see in each one of us. Instead, we are the reluctant ones. Even as you prepare to give yourself to us, we find it hard to give ourselves to one another. Even as you invite us to your table, we still are seeking our own possessions and gifts. Forgive us, and grant that we may eat at your table tonight as ones renewed as your disciples, so that this occasion may be for us not only a time of sorrow for our sin, but also a way to anticipate your celebration of a life of joy. Amen.

| | |
|---|---|
| **LEADER:** | Jesus came to them saying, "I have earnestly desired to eat this passover with you, for I will not eat of it again until the Kingdom of God is fulfilled." So he sent them into the city, saying . . . |
| **ALL:** | Go into the city and a man carrying a jar of water will meet you; follow him, and at the place he enters say to the householder, "Where is my guest room, where I am to eat the passover with my disciples?" He will show you a room furnished and ready; there prepare for us. |
| **LEADER:** | And they went their way. |
| **READER 1:** | Everything is arranged just as he said. |
| **READER 2:** | My feet are burning. What a day! I wish I had the energy of Peter. At least we won't have to eat fish. |

| | |
|---|---|
| **READER 3:** | Did someone mention my name? Don't worry; we will eat soon, and a meal better than any catch of fish. |
| **READER 4:** | Thank heaven. Fish are dwindling away anyway this season and the quality is not very good either. |
| **READER 5:** | Thomas, if I listened to you much, I wouldn't ever cast a net! |
| **READER 6:** | I admire Thomas. He may be a skeptic but that's better than being an impractical dreamer like some of you. |
| **READER 7:** | Like Nathaniel. Always seeing things unseen. Like this room. Can you see what is left undone? There is a lot to do and soon everyone will be here. |
| **READER 8:** | Such disorganization! I'm glad I never kept my tax ledgers like this! |
| **LEADER:** | So much to be done. So little time for all of us. So much to get ready. Do we take the time? Let us pray. |
| **ALL:** | Gracious God, thank you for bread and for the fruit of the vine. Thank you for Christ the most precious gift of all, who has drawn us together into unity with him and has won for us a victory over sin and death. May we by his victory set out to unravel the mysteries of our own talents as we serve him, and may we concentrate our lives on him alone. May these gifts tonight be consecrated to that purpose so that we turn from all denial or betrayal of him toward becoming signs of our renewed covenant and faith, until we drink and eat at last with him in his kingdom. Amen. |
| **LEADER:** | As they gathered for the meal, he began to teach them, saying, |
| **TABLES 1 AND 7:** | "I am the vine and God is the vinedresser. Every branch that bears no fruit, God takes away, and every branch that bears fruit, God prunes so that it will bear more fruit." |
| **TABLES 2 AND 8:** | "If the world hates you, know that it hated me before it hated you. If you were of this world, the world would love you as its own, but because you are not of the world, the world hates you." |
| **TABLES 3 AND 9:** | "I have called you friends. You did not choose me. I chose you and appointed you to go and bear fruit. This I command you, to love one another." |
| **TABLES 4 AND 10:** | "As God loved me, so have I loved you. If you keep my commandments, you will abide in my love, just as I have kept God's commandments and abide in God's love. I have told you these things so that my joy may be in you." |
| **TABLES 5 AND 11:** | "I did not say these things to you from the beginning, because I was with you. Now that I am going away, sorrow has filled your hearts." |

| | |
|---|---|
| **TABLES 6 AND 12:** | "When the Holy Spirit comes, the spirit will guide you into all truth." |
| **LEADER:** | He took the bread, lifted it up to heaven, and giving thanks, broke it, saying, "Take. Eat. This is my body given for you." |

*(The bread is distributed and broken at each table.)*

After supper he took the cup and said, "This is the blood of the new covenant, which is poured out for you. Drink this in remembrance of me."

*(The cup is distributed and poured at each table.)*

*Hymn: "Come, Sinners, to the Gospel Feast"*

*(The meal is shared.)*

And he began to say, "You will all fall away, for it is written, 'I will strike the shepherd, and the sheep will be scattered.' Behold, the hand of the one who betrays me is with us at this very table."

| | |
|---|---|
| **TABLES 1 AND 2:** | Could it be me? |
| **TABLES 3 AND 4:** | Is it I? |
| **TABLES 5 AND 6:** | Is it I? |
| **TABLES 7 AND 8:** | Am I the one? |
| **TABLES 9 AND 10:** | Or me? |
| **TABLES 11 AND 12:** | Or me? |

*(Lights go out and only the candles remain lit.)*

*Time of Silence*

*Pastoral Prayer*

*Hymn: " 'Tis Midnight and on Olive's Brow"*

| | |
|---|---|
| **LEADER:** | Our service is ended. Only the dim light of candles remains. Go forth in silence to ponder these things. |

# AN EASTER STORY

## Curt McCormack

**PRODUCTION NOTES:** This play is ideal for churches wishing to include many children in their production. All parts are short and easily learned. Parts are for ten children and one adult. If you have fewer children, simply combine parts. Children play themselves; when speaking to them, use their names rather than "Speaker." No special costumes or props are needed.

*(DIRECTOR begins reading the resurrection story from Matthew 28. Is interrupted by SPEAKER 1.)*

**SPEAKER 1:** Director *(or use person's name),* Oh Director, isn't this the place where the Easter Bunny jumps out and leaves Easter eggs for everybody?

**DIRECTOR:** No, Speaker 1, this is not where the Easter Bunny comes out and leaves colored eggs . . . there is no Easter Bunny in this story!

**SPEAKER 1:** What! No Easter Bunny? Then how can it possibly be an Easter story?

**SPEAKER 2:** We wanna hear the story about the Easter Bunny! *(All the children exclaim yes, or some other affirming remark. Then they all begin to chant, We want the Easter Bunny . . . etc.)*

**DIRECTOR:** Now just a minute! I'm starting to tell you the Easter story. The real Easter story. It's not about Easter bunnies . . . it's about Jesus.

**SPEAKER 3:** Didn't Jesus believe in the Easter Bunny?

**DIRECTOR:** Well . . . no . . . *(interrupted by children)*

**ALL:** *(ad lib)* Jesus didn't believe in the Easter Bunny? Didn't Jesus like bunnies?

**DIRECTOR:** Yes, of course, Jesus likes bunnies . . . but there was no Easter Bunny when Jesus lived on earth. The Easter Bunny hadn't been invented yet.

**SPEAKER 4:** What do you mean, he hadn't been invented yet?

**SPEAKER 5:** *(should be a girl)* Just a minute! What do you mean "he" . . . what makes you think the Easter Bunny is a he? Huh?

| | |
|---|---|
| **DIRECTOR:** | Now hold it kids! Let's settle down for a moment. The Easter Bunny is a fairly modern concept. However, people have been coloring eggs for a long, long time. Matter of fact, a story is told that many years ago . . . |
| **SPEAKER 6:** | How many years ago? *(Others respond.)* Yeah, how many? |
| **DIRECTOR:** | It's hard to say exactly . . . maybe 200 or so . . . anyway, suppos-edly an old German woman wanted to give gifts to her children in honor of Easter, but since she was poor, the only thing she had in the house was a few eggs. So she boiled them, colored them, and hid them outside in the tall grass. When the children found them the children saw a bunny hopping away as if the bunny had left the eggs. From that came the story that the bunny had left the eggs. It was later adapted into the Easter tradition. |
| **SPEAKER 7:** | I don't know if I want to believe that or not . . . so, why do we color eggs on Easter? |
| **DIRECTOR:** | A good question. If I recall, the custom of coloring and giving eggs as gifts goes back to Egypt, hundreds of years before Jesus was born, possibly even before Moses. Eggs represented something very special. Do you happen to know what that might have been? |
| **SPEAKER 8:** | Breakfast? |
| **DIRECTOR:** | Uhhhh . . . no, but they may have eaten them for breakfast. |
| **SPEAKER 9:** | I'll bet they gave colored eggs to people who were going to have a baby. After all, babies come from eggs, right? |
| | *(The children all laugh and start to make fun of SPEAKER 9).* |
| **DIRECTOR:** | Now just a minute, Speaker 9 is almost right! It does have to do with birth. Eggs have always been a symbol of new life, new hope, and new possibilities. The church liked the idea and thought it went very well with the meaning of the resurrection, so the church borrowed it. |
| **SPEAKER 10:** | You say that the egg represents new life. Well, if that's true, and Easter is supposed to be about Jesus being . . . rezurcocted . . . raser . . . rizz . . . what's the word? |
| **DIRECTOR:** | Do you mean resurrected? |
| **SPEAKER 10:** | Yes, that's it. If Easter is about Jesus being resurrected . . . com-ing back to life, then eggs and Easter do have something in com-mon don't they? |
| **DIRECTOR:** | Indeed they do. The egg still represents new life and Jesus' resur-rection symbolizes new life and new possibilities. Jesus lives! is a great Easter message isn't it? |

| | |
|---|---|
| **ALL:** | Yes! *(shouting)* Jesus lives! *(repeat)* |
| **SPEAKER 1:** | So what about the Easter Bunny? Is he real or not? |
| **DIRECTOR:** | Think for a moment. Do rabbits lay eggs? |
| **SPEAKER 1:** | I don't think so. Hey! they don't. Well, if the Easter Bunny is not real, how do we know that Santa Claus is real? |
| **DIRECTOR:** | Santa is a story for another day. We're talking about Easter. The bunny is a nice symbol of Easter. . . . A warm, cuddly, fluffy bunny rabbit . . . is a special part of the Easter tradition for many people. But the colored eggs are a more important symbol for us—a symbol of the empty tomb, where Jesus was . . . no more! And why is that? |
| **ALL:** | Because he lives! |
| **DIRECTOR:** | Let's read the story of Easter now, shall we? |

*(Play ends with reading.)*

# THE GUARDIANS

## Kevin Stone

**PURPOSE:** To remind us that we have a living Lord who has conquered death. To emphasize God's power and the foolishness of standing in God's way. To encourage sacrificial dedication to Jesus Christ.
**LENGTH:** 6 to 7 minutes.
**PRODUCTION NOTES:** A comedy sketch for Easter, or for any other time when the Resurrection is remembered.

The "stone" is imaginary, and is located down center. This way, the guards can look at the audience when looking at the tomb. (And the audience can experience being buried with Christ and rising with him—see Romans 6:4-5 and Colossians 2:12.)

New on the job, CLIFFORD is aloof and very nervous. He tries almost too hard. The CHIEF is abrupt and overbearing when venting his frustration, but he quickly subsides into his normal serene state of boredom. He's done hundreds of security jobs, and this is just one more.

Modern security uniforms would be perfect attire. The only props needed are two spears and something to sit on.

The strobe should be placed down center so that it shines from the direction of the tomb. The music will need to be a short, invigorating piece (10 to 20 seconds long).

*(CLIFFORD is vigilant; he clumsily marches back and forth with wary eyes and a set mouth; he starts as if hearing a sound and slowly moves downstage, spear ready, scanning the audience suspiciously; satisfied, he resumes his march; CHIEF enters.)*

| | |
|---|---|
| **CLIFFORD:** | *(Spinning around, he brings the CHIEF to a halt with the point of his spear.)* Prepare to die, grave robber! |
| **CHIEF:** | *(unruffled)* Where do you get those corny lines? |
| **CLIFFORD:** | *(dropping his spear and hastily trying to smooth out his boss's uniform)* Oh! Oh! I'm sorry, Chief! Really I am. |
| **CHIEF:** | *(brushing him aside)* I wish you'd quit trying to kill me every time I walk up. Do I *look* like a grave robber? |

12

| | |
|---|---|
| **CLIFFORD:** | Well, I've, uh—never actually seen one. |
| **CHIEF:** | *(losing patience)* Where's my shovel? Tell me that! |
| **CLIFFORD:** | Uh—in your tool shed? |
| **CHIEF:** | I don't have it with me! That's the point! Why would a grave robber come without a shovel? *(looks at the stone)* 'Course, it'd take more than a shovel to get through *that*. |
| **CLIFFORD:** | Well, I recognize you now . . . |
| **CHIEF:** | About time. This is our third day workin' together. *(sits)* Ah, the sun'll be up in a few minutes. Maybe you can see a little more clearly then. |
| | *(CLIFFORD picks up his spear and resolutely marches again.)* |
| | Look, kid, I know this is your first assignment and all, but you gotta relax. |
| **CLIFFORD:** | *(shrilly)* I'm relaxed! |
| **CHIEF:** | If *that's* relaxed, then I'm Tiberius Caesar. *(stands)* This isn't good for you. You've been all tensed up for three days now. |
| **CLIFFORD:** | What do you want me to do? |
| **CHIEF:** | Stop marchin' around like that for one thing. *(He stops.)* Now, you got a hold of that spear there like you're tryin' to strangle the thing. Unclench your fist some . . . nice loose grip. There. Isn't it nice when you can feel your fingers? *(CLIFFORD gives a short nod.)* Now we'll get the rest of you loosened up. *(CHIEF stands to the right of CLIFFORD, both of them fully facing the audience.)* Take a deep breath . . . |
| | *(CHIEF takes a breath and slowly exhales, then notices that CLIFFORD is still holding his in.)* |
| | Uh, you can let it out now. |
| | *(CLIFFORD noisily expels his breath.)* |
| **CLIFFORD:** | Thanks. |
| **CHIEF:** | O.K., relax your neck . . . |
| | *(CHIEF lets his head hang down; CLIFFORD does the same.)* |
| | Relax your shoulders . . . |
| | *(CHIEF loosens his shoulders, letting his arms hang freely; CLIFFORD follows the example.)* |
| | Relax everything . . . |
| | *(CLIFFORD falls to the ground in a heap; CHIEF looks at him, then says to the audience:)* |

You gotta feel sorry for the guy. *(He stoops and drags him up.)* Clifford, c'mon.

| | |
|---|---|
| **CLIFFORD:** | How'd I do, Chief? |
| **CHIEF:** | You tell me. How do you feel? |
| **CLIFFORD:** | *(apprehensively)* Like something's gonna happen. |
| **CHIEF:** | *(exasperated)* What's here that you're so uptight about? |
| **CLIFFORD:** | I dunno. |
| **CHIEF:** | We've got a tomb. Inside the tomb is a *what*? |
| **CLIFFORD:** | A—a body? |
| **CHIEF:** | You're right! Of a man who's been dead since Friday. Hasn't moved a muscle, has he? |

*(CLIFFORD shrugs and shakes his head. CHIEF moves down stage to the stone)*

And—what is this?

| | |
|---|---|
| **CLIFFORD:** | It's a rock. |
| **CHIEF:** | *Big* rock, Clifford. *Big* rock. *Heavy* rock. And it's sealed—see that? *(He pats the stone.)* Nobody's movin' this thing. Especially with *us* here! We're security guards! |
| **CLIFFORD:** | *(still nervous)* Yeah. Everything's under control. |
| **CHIEF:** | Now you're talkin'. This is like a paid vacation. *(sits)* Now if you said this was a *strange* assignment, I'd agree with you. Been doin' security for twenty years. Never thought I'd spend three days sitting by a rock guarding a dead man. What I like is some excitement! A good tough job—like Barabbas. Did I tell you I guarded Barabbas? |
| **CLIFFORD:** | The murderer? |
| **CHIEF:** | Oh, let's see—murder, robbery, sedition, insurrection—you name it, he did it. He was tough. And talk about a bad attitude! I think he hated everybody. |
| **CLIFFORD:** | Why'd they let him go? |
| **CHIEF:** | Huh. Beats me. They let him go free, and then—*(He gestures toward the stone.)* they kill *this* guy. Don't make much sense. |
| **CLIFFORD:** | I bet Barabbas is glad. |
| **CHIEF:** | He oughta be. The only reason he's alive today is because this fellow took his place. You'd think that'd make *anybody* glad. |

*(pause)*

| | |
|---|---|
| **CLIFFORD:** | Chief? |
| **CHIEF:** | I'm right here, Clifford. |
| **CLIFFORD:** | You're sure nothing can happen? |
| **CHIEF:** | As sure as the sun's gonna rise. You're not getting nervous again, are you? |
| **CLIFFORD:** | Well, the chief priests thought his followers might try to—you know, come and steal him or something. |
| **CHIEF:** | Humph! I don't know why those chief priests are so paranoid. Did you notice it when you talked to them? |
| **CLIFFORD:** | They were upset. I thought it was because of their curtain. |
| **CHIEF:** | What curtain? |
| **CLIFFORD:** | The curtain in the temple. Somebody tore it. |
| **CHIEF:** | Yeah, that'd make 'em mad, all right. Anything about their temple makes 'em mad. Like when this guy said to destroy it. That really got 'em. |
| **CLIFFORD:** | Destroy the temple? |
| **CHIEF:** | That's what he said. And in three days he'd raise it back up. Of course, nobody could do that in three days, but it scared those priests. They're paranoid. I've never seen people so edgy . . . except you. *(He stands and paces.)* |
| **CLIFFORD:** | I heard his followers are dangerous. |
| **CHIEF:** | Dangerous? Ha! Harmless as doves! I know for a *fact*—they ran a dozen different directions when he got arrested. One of them came and watched him die, but nobody's even seen *him* since Friday. |
| **CLIFFORD:** | Maybe they're planning an attack! |
| **CHIEF:** | Yeah, right. They're scared to death somebody's gonna come crucify *them* next. |
| **CLIFFORD:** | But, if they were loyal to him . . . |
| **CHIEF:** | Ha! Loyalty only goes so far, buddy. People will follow right up until the time it starts to hurt, and then—*bang!* They're gone! We'll probably never see any of 'em again. |
| **CLIFFORD:** | I suppose you're right. |
| **CHIEF:** | *(shrugs)* He's dead. That changes things. |
| | *(CLIFFORD sighs and fidgets.)* |

| | |
|---|---|
| CHIEF: | Hey, first assignment. Rookie jitters. |
| CLIFFORD: | *(pacing)* No, really, it's not that. |
| CHIEF: | I just don't see how anybody can be nervous on a job as easy as this. Look around—you got the flowers, they're bloomin'. You got the birds, they're, uh—*(He stops, puzzled.)* |
| CLIFFORD: | No—they aren't singing. I haven't heard one since Friday, when we had the earthquake and it got so dark. Something's wrong. . . |

*(pause)*

| | |
|---|---|
| CHIEF: | *(breaking the tension with a hearty laugh)* Well, who says birds can't take a break every now and then? This is the weekend, you know! Can't expect 'em to sing all the time! |

*(Sound effects: a low rumble)*

| | |
|---|---|
| CLIFFORD: | *(very tense)* Did you hear that? |
| CHIEF: | Hear what? |
| CLIFFORD: | I don't know. . . |

*(Sound effects: louder rumble)*

*(CLIFFORD stumbles and drops his spear; CHIEF staggers to his left one step.)*

*That's* what I heard.

| | |
|---|---|
| CHIEF: | Hey, probably just some aftershocks from Friday! |
| CLIFFORD: | *(picking up his spear in awe)* Aftershocks!—of course! It just dawned on me! |
| CHIEF: | *(looking at the sky)* Yeah, it's dawn all right— |
| CLIFFORD: | *(counting on his fingers)* Friday-Saturday-Sunday! He's rebuilding the temple! |
| CHIEF: | *(still looking at the sky)* Here comes the sunrise! |

*(Sound effects: very loud rumbling: earthquake)*

*(They both stumble and fall; they get back up, trying hard to maintain their balance; LIGHTS out, STROBE on, MUSIC up; CLIFFORD and CHIEF, grasping each other to maintain balance, stare at the stone and scream in terror; they both fall down flat; SOUND EFFECTS fade out; STROBE off, LIGHTS fade up; MUSIC fade out; CLIFFORD and CHIEF both "come to" and slowly sit up, staring at the stone.)*

*(blankly)* This changes things.

**CLIFFORD:** *(standing)* Maybe . . . maybe we can roll the stone back—oh no . . . no . . . we can't hide this . . . there's no way . . . how are we ever going to *explain* this?

**CHIEF:** This changes things.

**CLIFFORD:** *(pulling him to his feet)* C'mon, get up.

**CHIEF:** This changes *everything*.

*(Sound effects: birds singing, up and under)*

**CLIFFORD:** *(moving toward exit)* You know we're gonna lose our jobs for this!

**CHIEF:** *(snapping out of his bewilderment and following him)* Don't look at me! I *told* you something like this would happen! But would you listen? No-o-o-o!

*(Exit both.)*

*(Sound effects: birds, up and fade out)*

*(Lights out)*

# WHERE IS THE PROOF?

**Richard Poteet**

**SETTING:** A courtroom with judge's bench, witness stand, and chairs and tables for two attorneys. The audience, or congregation, is the jury. Witnesses are seated in the audience. All cast characters are dressed in modern attire, since ancient Palestinian dress would tend to make the jury spectators instead of participants in the play. Time: several weeks following the resurrection of Jesus.

**CAST:**

CLAUDIUS MARCELLUS, Judge
CORNELIUS FLAVIUS, Attorney for the affirmative case
ANTONIUS GAIUS, Attorney for the negative case
BAILIFF
MARY MAGDALENE
SIMON PETER
BARTHOLOMEW CLEOPAS
NATHANAEL THOMAS
JUSTIN MARCUS
THE JURY

*(The attorneys and BAILIFF are seated in the courtroom as the play begins. The judge enters from an adjoining room.)*

**BAILIFF:** *(standing, facing the jury, as the judge enters)* The court will please rise. *(after audience rises)* The 102nd District Court of the Roman Empire is now in session. The Honorable Claudius Marcellus presiding. *(after judge is seated)* You may be seated.

**JUDGE:** I will remind the court that this session is a hearing. We are here to determine whether or not Jesus of Nazareth arose from the dead as has been claimed. We will hear the testimony and evidence of the affirmative case as it will be presented by Mr. Cornelius Flavius on my right *(FLAVIUS stands.)*; and the testimony and evidence of the negative case as it will be presented by Mr. Antonius Gaius on my left *(GAIUS stands.)*. Are you gentlemen ready to proceed?

| | |
|---|---|
| **FLAVIUS AND GAIUS:** | We are, Your Honor. *(They are then seated.)* |
| **JUDGE:** | Bailiff . . . you will now swear in the jury. |
| **BAILIFF:** | *(standing in front of the jury and in monotone voice)* The jury will please rise. *(after jury rises)* Do you, the members of this jury, solemnly swear to render a faithful hearing to the testimony now to be presented to this court; and do you promise to render a fair and just verdict according to this testimony and evidence? If so, please let it now be known by saying, "We do." *(after jury responds)* You may be seated. |
| **JUDGE:** | We will now hear the opening remarks of the attorneys. I will remind you that your remarks should be brief and to the point, stating to the court the intent of your case. We shall begin with Mr. Flavius, representing the affirmative case. |
| **FLAVIUS:** | *(standing and facing the jury)* Thank you, Your Honor. I shall argue that Jesus of Nazareth, hailed by many to be the Messiah, arose from the dead on *(Easter date),* three days following his death on *(Good Friday date).* I shall show that this event is an authentic fact, and documented by eyewitness accounts. Thank you. *(He sits.)* |
| **JUDGE:** | Mr. Gaius. |
| **GAIUS:** | *(standing, facing the jury)* I wish to inform the court that I shall prove to you, beyond the shadow of a doubt, that the alleged resurrection of this Jesus of Nazareth is a hoax, and the creation of the minds of biased individuals. I shall contend that this resurrection is nothing more than the fabrication of the imagination and totally alien to the truth. Thank you. |
| **JUDGE:** | We shall now proceed to the testimony of the witnesses. Mr. Flavius, we shall begin with your witnesses. |
| **FLAVIUS:** | Your Honor, I call Mary Magdalene to the stand. |
| **BAILIFF:** | Mary Magdalene to the stand. *(She comes forward from the audience and stands by the witness chair.)* Raise your right hand. State your name. |
| **MARY MAGDALENE:** | Mary Magdalene. |
| **BAILIFF:** | Do you solemnly swear to tell the truth, the whole truth, and nothing but the truth? |
| **MARY:** | I do. |

| | |
|---|---|
| **BAILIFF:** | You may be seated. |
| **FLAVIUS:** | Miss Magdalene, would you tell the court what happened to you on the morning of *(Easter date)?* |
| **MARY:** | Some friends and I went to the tomb where Jesus was buried to take some spices and flowers. When we arrived, we discovered that the stone covering the tomb was rolled away and his body was gone. We were very upset because we were afraid the Romans had taken his body. Suddenly an angel appeared and told us that Jesus had arisen from the dead. He commanded us to go tell his disciples that Jesus was alive. As we ran, suddenly we saw Jesus himself. |
| **FLAVIUS:** | Did he speak to you? |
| **MARY:** | Yes. He said: "Mary, don't be afraid. Go tell my disciples that I am alive, that you have seen me, and that I will meet them in Galilee." |
| **FLAVIUS:** | So you actually saw and heard Jesus on *(Easter date)?* |
| **MARY:** | Yes. |
| **FLAVIUS:** | No more questions, Your Honor. |
| **JUDGE:** | Mr. Gaius, do you wish to cross-examine this witness? |
| **GAIUS:** | Yes, Your Honor. Miss Magdalene, did you ever have a previous encounter with Jesus before your stated meeting on *(Easter date)?* |
| **MARY:** | Yes. |
| **GAIUS:** | Would you tell the court the nature of this encounter? |
| **MARY:** | Several months ago my whole life was changed by Jesus. You see, up until that time I had been very unstable and I had lost all control of myself. I was brought to Jesus by some friends, and he restored my health to me. |
| **GAIUS:** | You were mentally ill? |
| **MARY:** | *(hesitantly)* Well, yes, I suppose so. |
| **GAIUS:** | But now you say you are cured of this mental illness? |
| **MARY:** | Yes. |
| **GAIUS:** | So . . . we can assume that you had a vested interest in this man. He healed you . . . and you felt you owed him a debt. And because he did so much for you, is it not true that you would believe anything he said? |
| **FLAVIUS:** | Objection, Your Honor. That question calls for a conclusion on the part of the witness. |

| | |
|---|---|
| **JUDGE:** | Sustained. Rephrase your question, Mr. Gaius. |
| **GAIUS:** | Miss Magdalene, did you ever hear Jesus promise that he would be raised from the dead three days following his death? |
| **MARY:** | Yes. |
| **GAIUS:** | And did you believe that promise? |
| **MARY:** | Yes. |
| **GAIUS:** | Did you believe this before or after your mental illness? |
| **MARY:** | *(confused and puzzled)* . . . I don't know. |
| **GAIUS:** | One final question. Did you believe that Jesus was the Son of God? |
| **MARY:** | Yes! |
| **GAIUS:** | No more questions. |
| **JUDGE:** | The witness is dismissed. Mr. Flavius, you may call your next witness. |
| **FLAVIUS:** | I call Simon Peter to the stand. |
| **BAILIFF:** | Simon Peter to the stand. *(after SIMON PETER comes to the witness stand)* Raise your right hand. State your name. |
| **SIMON PETER:** | Simon Peter. |
| **BAILIFF:** | Do you promise to tell the truth, the whole truth, and nothing but the truth? |
| **PETER:** | I do. |
| **BAILIFF:** | Be seated. |
| **FLAVIUS:** | Simon Peter, would you tell the court what happened to you on *(Easter date)*. |
| **PETER:** | I got up early that morning and went down to the boat docks. Sentimental attachment, I guess. I went there to see the boat I once owned. I was very depressed that morning and felt the fresh air would do me good. Suddenly Mary Magdalene came running up to me screaming that Jesus had risen from the dead. At first I thought she was just having another hysterical episode, but then I decided it wouldn't hurt anything to go see for myself. Sure enough, when I started to think about it, I got excited, started to run, and discovered that the stone covering the tomb had been rolled away and he was gone. At first I blew up in anger thinking those Romans . . . uh, pardon me judge . . . someone had stolen his body. But then Mary told me that Jesus promised he would appear to us in Galilee. |

| | |
|---|---|
| **FLAVIUS:** | And did you go to Galilee? |
| **PETER:** | As fast as these tired old feet would carry me! |
| **FLAVIUS:** | And what happened there? |
| **PETER:** | We were all together at Andrew's house. After several hours of waiting and wondering, suddenly Jesus was there among us. |
| **FLAVIUS:** | Did he speak to you? |
| **PETER:** | Yes. He told us to go into all the world and preach the gospel. |
| **FLAVIUS:** | So you too actually saw and heard Jesus after *(Easter date)*? |
| **PETER:** | Yes. |
| **FLAVIUS:** | No more questions. |
| **JUDGE:** | Mr. Gaius. |
| **GAIUS:** | Simon Peter, what is your occupation? |
| **PETER:** | *(hesitant and surprised)* . . . Uh, I'm unemployed at the moment. |
| **GAIUS:** | *(sarcastically)* Have you *ever* been employed? |
| **PETER:** | Yes, I was a fisherman for twenty-three years. |
| **GAIUS:** | Were you *fired* from this occupation? |
| **PETER:** | No, I was self-employed. *(braggingly)* I found out as a boy that if I was worth five dollars to another man for a day's work, I was worth ten if I worked for myself. |
| **GAIUS:** | That's interesting. Why then did you give up your work? |
| **PETER:** | About three years ago Jesus came down to the docks, asked me to follow him, and I did. |
| **GAIUS:** | *(with astonishment)* You mean you just gave up everything and followed a total stranger? |
| **PETER:** | *(proudly)* Yes. |
| **GAIUS:** | So . . . we can assume that you, too, had a vested interest in this man. In fact, you gave up everything—family, possessions, your profession—but he kinda' let you down didn't he? |
| **PETER:** | No, he didn't. He arose from the dead and fixed you Romans! |
| **JUDGE:** | *(with a pound of the gavel)* The witness will confine himself to answering the questions of the counselor. |
| **GAIUS:** | So . . . with all that you had invested in this man, it is understandable that you would want to believe that he arose from the dead—else he would be a failure, and you too would be a failure. |

| | |
|---|---|
| **FLAVIUS:** | Your Honor, I object. The counselor is again calling for a conclusion on the part of the witness. |
| **JUDGE:** | Sustained. |
| **GAIUS:** | I shall rephrase my question, Your Honor. Simon Peter, did you ever hear Jesus promise that he would be raised from the dead? |
| **PETER:** | Yes. |
| **GAIUS:** | And did you believe that promise? |
| **PETER:** | Yes. |
| **GAIUS:** | If then he did not arise from the dead, would he not be a liar? |
| **PETER:** | *(reluctantly)* I . . . I guess so. |
| **GAIUS:** | Simon Peter, did you believe that Jesus was the Son of God? |
| **PETER:** | *(strongly)* He *was* and *is* the Son of God! |
| **GAIUS:** | *(quickly)* Have you *always* felt this way? |
| **PETER:** | *(nervously)* . . . Uh . . . yes. |
| **GAIUS:** | *(boldly)* ARE YOU SURE? *(Peter becomes nervous and does not answer.)* IS IT NOT TRUE THAT ON THE EVENING OF *(Good Friday date)* YOU DENIED YOU EVEN KNEW HIM AND YOU MADE THIS DENIAL NOT ONCE BUT *THREE* TIMES? |
| **PETER:** | *(nervously)* Yes, but . . . |
| **GAIUS:** | *(quickly)* How did you feel after these denials? |
| **PETER:** | *(after a pause and quietly)* I was sorry for what I'd done. |
| **GAIUS:** | You felt guilty. |
| **PETER:** | Yes. |
| **GAIUS:** | *(after a pause)* Simon Peter, from time to time all of us say things about someone that we later regret, especially if that person dies. We wish we could take it back, but we can't. We wish that person were alive again so we could apologize and absolve our guilt. |
| **FLAVIUS:** | *(angrily)* Your Honor, really now! This whole line of questioning is totally irrelevant. I object. |
| **JUDGE:** | Mr. Gaius, would you like to explain to the court your intent with such questioning? |
| **GAIUS:** | I withdraw the question, Your Honor. I'm finished with this witness. |
| **JUDGE:** | The witness is excused. Mr. Flavius. |
| **FLAVIUS:** | I call Bartholomew Cleopas to the stand. |

| | |
|---|---|
| **BAILIFF:** | Bartholomew Cleopas to the stand *(after Cleopas gets to the witness stand)* Raise your right hand. State your name. |
| **BARTHOLO-MEW CLEOPAS:** | Bartholomew Cleopas. |
| **BAILIFF:** | Do you solemnly swear to tell the truth, the whole truth, and nothing but the truth? |
| **CLEOPAS:** | I do. |
| **FLAVIUS:** | Mr. Cleopas, would you tell the court what happened to you on the afternoon of *(Easter date)*. |
| **CLEOPAS:** | A friend and I were walking from Jerusalem to my home in Emmaus. We were very saddened that day about what had happened. |
| **FLAVIUS:** | Referring to the crucifixion of Jesus? |
| **CLEOPAS:** | Yes. |
| **FLAVIUS:** | Then what happened? |
| **CLEOPAS:** | Suddenly a stranger joined us on the road and asked us what we were talking about. We told him about all that had happened in Jerusalem. We had no idea who he was until we asked him to have supper with us in my home. Then, as we sat around the table, we saw his hands—they were scarred where nails had pierced them. |
| **FLAVIUS:** | Did he tell you who he was? |
| **CLEOPAS:** | Yes. He said, "I am the one you have been talking about." |
| **FLAVIUS:** | Meaning Jesus of Nazareth? |
| **CLEOPAS:** | Yes. |
| **FLAVIUS:** | No more questions. |
| **JUDGE:** | Mr. Gaius. |
| **GAIUS:** | Mr. Cleopas, do you believe that Jesus was the Son of God? |
| **CLEOPAS:** | Yes. |
| **GAIUS:** | Did you ever have any personal contact with Jesus before your stated meeting on *(Easter date)*? |
| **CLEOPAS:** | No. I heard him teach from a distance, but I never really met him personally until *(Easter date)*. |
| **GAIUS:** | *(quickly, cynically)* So when this stranger walks up to you and tells you he's Jesus of Nazareth, you just assume he's telling the truth? |

| | |
|---|---|
| **CLEOPAS:** | Yes, but there were the wounds on his hands . . . |
| **GAIUS:** | *(quickly)* No more questions, Your Honor. |
| **JUDGE:** | The witness is excused. You may call your next witness, Mr. Flavius. |
| **FLAVIUS:** | I have one final witness, Your Honor. I call Nathanael Thomas to the stand. |
| **BAILIFF:** | Nathanael Thomas to the stand. *(after THOMAS arrives)* Raise your right hand. State your name. |
| **NATHANAEL THOMAS:** | Nathanael Thomas. |
| **BAILIFF:** | Do you promise to tell the truth, the whole truth, and nothing but the truth? |
| **THOMAS:** | I do. |
| **BAILIFF:** | Be seated. |
| **FLAVIUS:** | Mr. Thomas, would you tell the court what happened to you after the death of Jesus on *(Good Friday date)*. |
| **THOMAS:** | Well, I was very disillusioned and disappointed after the execution. I had followed Jesus for several years, and I was convinced that I had finally found the Messiah. But after the crucifixion I began to wonder if the whole thing had just been a hoax. I then began to seek employment. |
| **FLAVIUS:** | Would you tell the court what happened to you ten days later. |
| **THOMAS:** | Before that day, I heard wild rumors that Jesus had risen from the dead and had appeared to some of the disciples. Then two of the disciples found me and told me they had actually seen him. At first I had my doubts—I just didn't want to get involved and disillusioned again. I told them I would have to see the wounds on his hands and feet and place my hands on those wounds before I would believe it. They had a tough time convincing me, but they finally persuaded me to go with them to Galilee where they said Jesus would appear to them. |
| **FLAVIUS:** | And did you go to Galilee? |
| **THOMAS:** | Yes. And I shall never forget it. We were all together in Andrew's house, and suddenly Jesus was there. |
| **FLAVIUS:** | What happened then? |
| **THOMAS:** | *(slowly)* Jesus walked up to me . . . stretched out his hands and placed my hands in his. |

| | |
|---|---|
| **FLAVIUS:** | You actually touched Jesus ten days after his death. |
| **THOMAS:** | Yes. |
| **FLAVIUS:** | Did he say anything to you? |
| **THOMAS:** | Yes. He said, "Thomas, because you have seen me, you have believed. Blessed are those who have not seen, and yet believe." |
| **FLAVIUS:** | *(slowly and with conviction)* You saw him with your eyes. You heard him with your ears. You touched him with your hands. |
| **THOMAS:** | Yes. |
| **FLAVIUS:** | No more questions, Your Honor. |
| **JUDGE:** | Mr. Gaius. |
| **GAIUS:** | *(defeatedly after a pause)* Mr. Thomas, do you believe that Jesus is the Son of God? |
| **THOMAS:** | Yes. |
| **GAIUS:** | No more questions. |
| **JUDGE:** | The witness is excused. Mr. Flavius, I believe this was your last witness. |
| **FLAVIUS:** | Yes, Your Honor. |
| **JUDGE:** | Then you may call your first witness, Mr. Gaius. |
| **GAIUS:** | Your Honor, I have only one witness. I call First Sergeant Justin Marcus to the stand. |
| **BAILIFF:** | First Sergeant Justin Marcus to the stand. *(after MARCUS arrives at the stand)* Raise your right hand. State your name. |
| **JUSTIN MARCUS:** | Justin Marcus. |
| **BAILIFF:** | Do you promise to tell the truth, the whole truth, and nothing but the truth? |
| **MARCUS:** | I do. |
| **BAILIFF:** | Be seated. |
| **GAIUS:** | Sergeant Marcus, what is your occupation? |
| **MARCUS:** | I am a First Sergeant in the 34th regiment of the Roman Army. |
| **GAIUS:** | Would you now tell the court where you were on the evening of *(day before Easter)*. |
| **MARCUS:** | I was posted as a guard at the tomb of Jesus of Nazareth. |

| | |
|---|---|
| **GAIUS:** | Why were you assigned to this post? |
| **MARCUS:** | I was assigned to this post by Pontius Pilate, who was warned that some of the disciples of Jesus might try to steal the body from the tomb. |
| **GAIUS:** | Sergeant, your record in the services of the Roman Army has been above repute. While I do not intend to incriminate that record, I feel it necessary to ask you the following question: While you were on duty that night, were you fully awake and alert during the entire evening? |
| **MARCUS:** | No, as a matter of fact I wasn't. You see, I had been on guard duty the night before and didn't get much sleep. During the night I dozed off for a couple of hours. |
| **GAIUS:** | What happened when you awakened? |
| **MARCUS:** | I discovered that the stone had been rolled away and the body of Jesus was gone. |
| **GAIUS:** | Is it possible that someone could have taken the body from the tomb while you were asleep that night? |
| **MARCUS:** | Yes. |
| **GAIUS:** | No more questions, Your Honor. |
| **JUDGE:** | Mr. Flavius, do you wish to cross-examine the witness? |
| **FLAVIUS:** | I certainly do, Your Honor. Sergeant, you testified that it was *possible* for someone to have taken the body from the tomb while you were asleep. |
| **MARCUS:** | That is correct. |
| **FLAVIUS:** | Sergeant, a lot of things are *possible*. It's possible that you could jump off the Temple in Jerusalem, isn't it? |
| **MARCUS:** | . . . Uh, I guess so. |
| **FLAVIUS:** | *(strongly)* I want to remind you, Sergeant, that in this court we are interested in *facts* and *not* vague possibilities. Are you able to give this court any *evidence* that someone actually took the body from the tomb? |
| **MARCUS:** | Well . . . no . . . but. . . |
| **FLAVIUS:** | Let's have a look at what actually happened. Were you present when the body of Jesus was placed inside the tomb? |
| **MARCUS:** | Yes. |
| **FLAVIUS:** | Were you present when the stone was rolled over the tomb to seal it? |

| | |
|---|---|
| **MARCUS:** | Yes. |
| **FLAVIUS:** | Did you roll the stone over by yourself? |
| **MARCUS:** | No. There were three other men that helped. |
| **FLAVIUS:** | Did you use any tools or instruments? |
| **MARCUS:** | Yes. We used some boards and chain. |
| **FLAVIUS:** | You testified that you fell asleep while guarding the tomb on *(night before Easter)*. How far away from the tomb were you when you fell asleep? |
| **MARCUS:** | *(reluctantly and quietly)* About five feet. |
| **FLAVIUS:** | Would you say that a little louder. I don't believe the jury heard you. |
| **MARCUS:** | About five feet. |
| **FLAVIUS:** | Five feet. That's not even as tall as you are, is it? |
| **MARCUS:** | No sir. |
| **FLAVIUS:** | One final question, Sergeant Marcus. Are you a heavy sleeper? |
| **GAIUS:** | Your Honor, counsel is purposely harassing the witness. |
| **FLAVIUS:** | I'll withdraw the question, Your Honor. I'm through with this witness *(cynically)*. |
| **JUDGE:** | The witness is excused. Mr. Gaius, did I understand that this is your only witness? |
| **GAIUS:** | That is correct, Your Honor. |
| **JUDGE:** | In that case we shall now hear the closing remarks. Mr. Gaius, you may begin. |
| **GAIUS:** | *(slowly)* Ladies and gentlemen of the jury, at the beginning of this hearing I stated my position that I would show you beyond the shadow of a doubt that the alleged resurrection of Jesus is a hoax, a fabrication of the imagination, and a claim that is totally alien to the truth. What you have seen here today is a firm documentation of my position. Now my colleague, Mr. Flavius, has paraded his so-called eyewitnesses before you—all claiming to have seen Jesus raised from the dead. But I warn the jury that there is one thing all these witnesses have in common—they all profess Jesus to be the Son of God. It is therefore evident that the testimony they have rendered has been slanted, biased, and clearly of a subjective nature. After investing their all in Jesus, they knew if he failed to arise from the dead, they too would be failures. So what we have in their testimony is not an objective and factual witness, |

but one that simply tells us what they *want* to believe. If Jesus is alive, he is alive only in the imaginations of those who *want* or *need* to believe it. Furthermore, I call your attention to the fact that my colleague failed to produce one witness that was not a part of this biased Christian group. Not one witness who could have given an objective testimony. Finally, I contend that the real issue here is that these Christians stole the body of Jesus in order to make this ridiculous claim that he is alive. His resurrection is utterly false, and I am sure you, members of the jury, who are much more interested in objective facts, will find this claim totally false. Thank you.

**JUDGE:** Mr. Flavius.

**FLAVIUS:** Ladies and gentlemen of the jury, my distinguished colleague, Mr. Gaius, would lead you to believe that the issue in this case is an empty tomb. This is *not* the real issue. The issue is whether or not Jesus is actually alive today. And *this* fact has been proved time and again by the eyewitness testimonies you have heard. I contend and base my entire case on these eyewitness testimonies. There is no need for me to enforce my case with other arguments, because these eyewitnesses alone bear out the truth in this case. I am certain that you too will see the truth as it is seen through those who know—those who saw him, heard him, touched him, and believe in him as the Son of God. Thank you.

**JUDGE:** Thank you, gentlemen. *(pause)* Before I dismiss the jury to deliberate your verdict, there are some things I feel I must say to you. Ordinarily, I do not follow such procedure, but I think the unusual nature of this case calls for it. You have heard both the affirmative and negative cases capably presented by Mr. Flavius and Mr. Gaius. However, I feel compelled to say that *neither* the affirmative *nor* the negative case is completely adequate to sustain a sound verdict. We have been dealing here with an issue that reaches beyond the limits of reasoning and law into the area of your own personal commitment as a jury. For this reason, I declare that there is insufficient evidence. I make this declaration because there is still one more witness to be heard before this question can be resolved. You yourselves are that witness. The remaining evidence to be presented can come only when you answer the question: "What evidence is there in my life that Jesus is alive?" So in the end, the issue at stake is not the absence of the dead, but the presence of the living. The verdict is yours. I now dismiss you to deliberate your verdict. Court is adjourned.

# SUNRISE

## Kevin Stone

**PURPOSE:** To present Jesus Christ as the sunrise in our dark world. To remind of a heaven where the sun never sets.

**LENGTH:** 3½ minutes.

**PRODUCTION NOTES:** This is a dramatic reading with music based on biblical references to the sun and its symbolism in scripture.

In several places, the verse being read is interrupted by an excerpt from another verse. This should be done in such a way that the audience follows the continuity of the original verse, but also catches the relevance of the other verse.

Ideally, Reader One is male and Reader Two is female. The reading can also be done by more than two readers, or by just one.

The overall tone of the piece is excitement. We see God's working in creation, the sending of the son, the Resurrection, and our heavenly home.

Scripture is adapted from the King James Version. Suggested music is "Psalm 57" from the album *Psalms Instrumental* (copyright © 1984 by Maranatha! Music).

*(Music up and under)*

**Reader 1:**    And God made two great lights; the greater light to rule the day, and the lesser light to rule the night. And God set them in the heaven to give light upon the earth.

**Reader 2:**    In the heaven he has set a tabernacle for the sun, which is like a bridegroom coming out of his chamber, and his going forth is from the end of the heaven; and there is nothing hid from the heat of it.

**Reader 1:**    In the cool of the day, they heard the voice of the Lord God walking in the garden, and they hid themselves from the presence of the Lord God amongst the trees of the garden. For all have sinned and come short of the glory of God.

*(pause)*

| | |
|---|---|
| **Reader 2:** | But unto you that fear my name shall the Sun of Righteousness arise with healing in his wings. |
| | And he shall be as the light of the morning, when the sun riseth, even a morning without clouds. |
| **Reader 1:** | I saw also the Lord sitting upon a throne, high and lifted up. |
| | And his countenance was as the sun shineth in his strength. |
| **Reader 2:** | Jesus brought them up unto a high mountain apart, and was transfigured before them: and his face did shine as the sun— |
| **Reader 1:** | Which is like a bridegroom coming out of his chamber. |
| **Reader 2:** | —And his raiment was white as the light. |
| **Reader 1:** | The friend of the bridegroom rejoices greatly because of the bridegroom's voice. This my joy therefore is fulfilled. |
| **Reader 2:** | The dayspring from on high hath visited us. |
| **Reader 1:** | Arise, shine, for thy light is come— |
| **Reader 2:** | —And the glory of the Lord is risen upon thee. |
| **Reader 1:** | God set them in heaven to give light upon the earth. |
| **Reader 2:** | Thy Word is a lamp unto my feet, and a light unto my path. |
| | *(pause)* |
| **Reader 1:** | Take heed, as unto a light in a dark place— |
| **Reader 2:** | —Until the day dawn, and the day star arise in your hearts. |
| | *(pause)* |
| **Reader 1:** | Why seek ye the living among the dead? He is not here; but he is risen! |
| **Reader 2:** | Unto you shall the Sun of Righteousness arise— |
| **Reader 1:** | He is not here; he is risen! |
| **Reader 2:** | —Arise, with healing in his wings! |
| **Reader 1:** | I go to prepare a place for you. |
| **Reader 2:** | And the city had no need of the sun to shine in it; for the glory of God did lighten it, and the Lamb is the light thereof— |
| **Reader 1:** | This my joy therefore is fulfilled! |
| **Reader 2:** | —And the nations of them which are saved shall walk in the light of it. |
| **Reader 1:** | And God made two great lights. |

**Reader 2:**      The sun shall no more be their light by day; neither for brightness shall the moon give light unto thee—

**Reader 1:**      —But the Lord shall be unto thee an everlasting light!

**Reader 2:**      And he shall be as the Light of the Morning, when the sun riseth.

**Reader 1:**      And there shall be no night there, and they need no candle, neither light of the sun, for the Lord God giveth them light—

**Readers 1 and 2:**      *(unison)* —And they shall reign forever and ever.

*(music out)*

# COME, HOLY SPIRIT

## A DRAMATIC WORSHIP FOR PENTECOST SUNDAY

### Georgianna Summers

**INTRODUCTION:** This service is designed for use in the church sanctuary for Pentecost Sunday. Before the service begins, eight red streamers, 36" x 5", cut from a silky, lightweight fabric into a flamelike shape, should be placed on the altar. They can be secured on the top of the altar with tape and allowed to hang down over the front.

The VERSE CHOIR is seated at the back of the sanctuary or in a balcony. Different voices in the VERSE CHOIR are designated by quality: light, medium, and dark. The CHOIR speaks at times solo, at times in unison. If possible, the person who reads the voice of GOD should speak over a microphone through a speaker system. The FOUR YOUTH, ADAM, WIFE, SON, and SPEAKER speak (unless otherwise designated in the script) from the front of the sanctuary. Their parts should be memorized.

Music adds to the effectiveness of the service. The organist or pianist should have at least one rehearsal with the VERSE CHOIR and cast to coordinate the music with the script.

Invocation, Hymn, Prayer, Offering precede this drama. The hymn included within the drama should be printed in the church bulletin. Instructions about singing it unannounced should be given to the congregation before the drama begins.

**PARTS:**
VERSE CHOIR (LIGHT, MEDIUM, DARK, SOLO, UNISON)
ADAM
WIFE
SON
SPEAKER
FOUR YOUTHS
GOD

## Part I: Where Are You?

*(Begin music suggesting the mysteriousness of creation. As it dies out, the VERSE CHOIR begins.)*

| | |
|---|---|
| **SOLO:** | God is spirit. |
| **UNISON:** | In the beginning God created the heavens and the earth. And the earth was without form, and darkness was upon the face of the deep. |
| **GOD:** | And the spirit of God was moving over the face of the waters. |
| | *(pause)* |
| **SOLO:** | God is light. |
| **UNISON:** | And God said, |
| **GOD:** | Let there be light! |
| **UNISON:** | And there was light. |
| | *(pause)* |
| **SOLO:** | God is power. |
| **UNISON:** | And from the same disk of gas that became the sun, the planets were born—whirling and spinning across the heavens, until one settled in orbit at the right place and the right distance—and God said, |
| **GOD:** | Let there be water—<br>And let the waters under the heavens be gathered into one place<br>And let the dry land appear. |
| **UNISON:** | And from the water there came—LIFE! |
| | *(The next nine lines should be spoken without pauses between.)* |
| **SOLO:** | Plants. |
| **SOLO:** | Fish. |
| **SOLO:** | Reptiles. |
| **SOLO:** | Birds. |
| **SOLO:** | Mammals. |
| **DARK:** | Life begetting life— |
| **MEDIUM:** | Each related to each— |
| **LIGHT:** | Each dependent on the other— |
| **UNISON:** | All stemming from a single source—God— |
| **SOLO:** | Is love. |
| **UNISON:** | Then God created human beings in God's own spiritual image. |
| **MEDIUM:** | Behold what manner of love the Creator has bestowed upon us that we should be called the children of God. |

| | |
|---|---|
| **UNISON:** | And God said, |
| **GOD:** | I have given you everything, but of the tree of the knowledge of good and evil you shall not eat—or you shall die! |
| **LIGHT:** | But the serpent said, |
| **SOLO:** | You will not die. Instead, your eyes will be opened, and you will be like God! |
| **UNISON:** | Like God! |
| | *(The next seven lines should be spoken without pauses between.)* |
| **SOLO:** | We shall have all knowledge— |
| **SOLO:** | All wisdom— |
| **SOLO:** | All power. |
| **MEDIUM:** | Power to run our own lives— |
| **LIGHT:** | To influence people— |
| **DARK:** | To control the world— |
| **UNISON:** | To conquer space! *(pause. Then start softly and build.)* Power, *Power,* POWER—WE SHALL BE LIKE GOD! *(pause)* So they disobeyed. *(pause)* Then—they heard the sound of God walking in the garden in the cool of the day. |
| **GOD:** | *(very loud)* Adam, Adam, where are you? *(FOUR YOUTHS in modern dress rise from aisle seats in different parts of the sanctuary, walk hurriedly to the chancel area as they say their lines, and then exit to the sides.)* |
| **YOUTH 1:** | Who's yelling at us? Can't they see we're busy? |
| **YOUTH 2:** | Yeah, I've gotta make it to track practice. |
| **YOUTH 3:** | And I have to get to work. I have to make some money. |
| **YOUTH 4:** | I've got studying to do. I have to go to college if I'm going to be a success. |
| **UNISON:** | Look at them, God. They don't need *you.* They're doing fine. |
| **GOD:** | *(a little softer)* Adam, Adam, where are you? |
| | *(ADAM and EVE rise up from congregation and come forward into the chancel area.)* |
| **ADAM:** | Here, God. Here in church. You should have known where to find us. We're the pillars. |
| **EVE:** | I'm on at least five committees, God, and an officer in everything. I really didn't want to be chair of that last dinner, but you know how it is, Lord. Nobody else would do it. It's such a shame that only a few of us will carry the load. |

35

| | |
|---|---|
| **ADAM:** | And I'm on the board and the finance committee. *(bragging)* Had the highest budget ever this year, Lord. Just think how great that's going to look on the annual report. |
| **SON:** | *(rising from the congregation and coming forward)* And have you noticed our youth group, God? I'm sure ours is the best in town. |
| **UNISON:** | Look what they've done for your church, Lord. Aren't you proud of them? |
| **GOD:** | *(a little softer)* Adam, Adam, where are you? |
| | *(ADAM and his family with the FOUR YOUTHS at the sides come together in the chancel area. A SPEAKER rises behind the pulpit. Can be the minister in pulpit robe.)* |
| **SPEAKER:** | Friends, a vote for Adam is a vote for a man who came up the hard way, a self-made man, a family man, steeped in good old-fashioned American morals. And he's a Christian. We've nothing to fear with the government in the hands of Adam. *(Group applauds. Then the FOUR YOUTHS leave to put on biblical robes for Part II. SPEAKER sits down behind pulpit and puts on robe if not already wearing one. SON turns his back to audience.)* |
| **GOD:** | *(softer still)* Adam, where are you? |
| **EVE:** | Adam, you've got to do something about Cain. He's impossible. Fights with his brother all the time. He won't listen to me. And I'm sure that crowd he runs around with is on drugs. |
| **ADAM:** | *(angrily)* You do something about him. You know I don't have time. How do you expect me to hold down a job, pay for the house, the boat, the cars—and take care of kids. That's your job. |
| **EVE:** | How much time do you think *I* have? I work too, you know, as well as helping with scouts, at the church, at school. |
| | *(Sound of gavel interrupts.)* |
| **SOLO:** | The divorce decree between Adam and his wife is hereby granted. *(EVE exits to one side of sanctuary. Sound of gavel again)* |
| **SOLO:** | Cain, I sentence you to life imprisonment—for murder! |
| | *(SON leaves down center aisle.)* |
| **GOD:** | *(barely audible)* Adam, Adam, where are you? *(ADAM drops to his knees at altar rail, head down, shoulders drooped.)* |
| **UNISON:** | In hell! Tormented by the evils of society. |
| | *(Next six lines to be spoken without pauses in between.)* |

| | |
|---|---|
| **SOLO:** | Divorce. |
| **SOLO:** | Violence. |
| **SOLO:** | Drugs. |
| **SOLO:** | Disease. |
| **SOLO:** | Terrorism. |
| **SOLO:** | Nuclear war. |
| **ADAM:** | *(in anguish, facing the altar)* They will destroy me! God, God, where are YOU? |
| | *(heavy, somber music as ADAM leaves)* |

## Part II: O Holy Spirit, Come!

| | |
|---|---|
| **UNISON:** | In the beginning was the Word, and the Word was God. |
| **LIGHT:** | In God was life, and the life was the light of humankind. |
| **DARK:** | The light shines in the darkness, and the darkness has not overcome it. |
| **MEDIUM:** | And the Word became flesh and dwelt among us. |
| **UNISON:** | No one has ever seen God; the only Son, he has made God known. |
| **SOLO:** | Now after Jesus had been crucified and his followers had experienced his risen presence, they returned to Jerusalem, and when the day of Pentecost had come, they were all together in one place. |
| | *(The FOUR YOUTHS wearing biblical robes come into chancel area. VERSE CHOIR makes mumbling noises simulating a group assembling. SPEAKER, wearing a robe, takes a place behind pulpit. Together they form the CHANCEL GROUP.)* |
| **SPEAKER:** | *(interrupting the mumbling. Voices gradually die out as SPEAKER's takes over.)* Friends, followers of the Way, we have come together once more to eat the Lord's Supper and to remember Jesus. |
| **YOUTH 1:** | Who does he think he is, always being the leader? Why doesn't he let someone else have a turn? |
| **YOUTH 2:** | Apollos is a good speaker. I think he would make a good leader. |
| **YOUTH 3:** | Oh no. Apollos is only a workman. He is not important enough to be the leader. |
| **YOUTH 4:** | And he is not really one of us. He is a Greek. Only Jews should be allowed to hold office. |
| | *(Half of VERSE CHOIR shouts "Yes, Yes!"; the other half, "No, No!")* |

| | |
|---|---|
| **YOUTH 1:** | I think only Jews should be allowed to belong at all. These Gentiles are immoral. They worship idols, eat unclean food. They can only be saved by obeying our Jewish law. |
| | *(Group in front and VERSE CHOIR all shout "Yes, Yes!" "No, No!")* |
| **SPEAKER:** | *(breaking in)* Friends, friends. We have come together to eat the Lord's Supper and to remember Jesus. |
| **YOUTH 2:** | Jesus is dead. He can no longer help us. |
| **YOUTH 3:** | No, he is not dead. There were those who saw him come out of the grave. |
| **YOUTH 4:** | Did you see him? |
| **YOUTH 3:** | No, but I know someone who did. |
| **YOUTH 4:** | I don't believe it. |
| **LIGHT:** | *(sing-song)* It's true. It's true. He was the Son of God, conceived by the Holy Spirit, born of the Virgin Mary. |
| **YOUTH 4:** | I don't believe that either. |
| **UNISON:** | *(gasp)* You cannot be one of us if you don't believe as we do. |
| **SPEAKER:** | Friends, friends, we have come together to *remember* Jesus, not to debate him. We must meet in harmony or we shall have no power. |
| **YOUTH 1:** | We have no power anyway. Who are we? |
| **UNISON:** | Nobody. A small group in an evil world. |
| **DARK:** | The Jews despise us. |
| **MEDIUM AND LIGHT:** | The Romans hate us. |
| **YOUTH 2:** | *(panic-stricken)* If we speak out they will destroy us. |
| **CHANCEL GROUP TOGETHER:** | What can we do? *(pause)* |
| **UNISON:** | Nothing. *(pause)* |
| **SPEAKER:** | *(with excitement)* That's it! *We* can do nothing, but God can do everything! Remember Jesus, how he entered the synagogue and read from Isaiah—"The Spirit of the Lord is upon me to preach good news to the poor, to release the captives, to open the eyes of the blind—" |
| **YOUTH 3:** | And how he said *we* would do even greater things. |

**YOUTH 4:** And how he promised that we should receive power when the Holy Spirit came upon us . . .

**SPEAKER:** And that we should be his witnesses to the ends of the earth!

**CHANCEL GROUP:** *(to one another)* When will this be? *(pause)*

**SPEAKER:** *(quietly)* When we seek it above all else.

**DARK:** Above wealth and fame and power.

**LIGHT:** *(questioning)* Above husband and wife and children and parents?

**MEDIUM:** *(questioning)* Above food and shelter and safety? *(pause)*

**SPEAKER:** Yes—remember how he said, "Seek *first* the kingdom of God."
Then—like a fire God's spirit will come
To warm our hearts and burn away our sins,
And like a mighty wind to blow us into flame,

**LIGHT:** And then 'twill catch from each to each,

**LIGHT AND MEDIUM:** Kindling the hearts of others,
Running over *their* dry, useless lives,

**UNISON:** Setting *them* aflame with light and *power* and LOVE!

*(pause. FOUR YOUTHS move to altar to kneel.)*

**SPEAKER:** *(fervently)* O Holy Spirit, come! Come upon us. *(sits)*

*(CHANCEL GROUP kneels at altar. They may kneel in silence for a moment, or the CHOIR or a soloist may sing a prayer hymn or anthem. Suggested anthem—"Come Down, Lord" by Stan Pethel, Hope Publishing Company, Carol Stream, IL 60188. If music is used, have a brief pause of expectation following it; then music, either live or taped, bursts forth to represent the coming of the Holy Spirit. Suggested music: First part of Bach's* Toccata *and* Fugue in D Minor. *As the music begins the FOUR YOUTHS rise and look around in wonder, then they turn to the altar, take a red streamer in each hand, and run through the congregation waving the streamers over the heads of the worshipers until the music dies out. They then exit to the back of the sanctuary to remove their biblical robes and return to modern dress for Part III.)*

**UNISON:** *(when YOUTHS have left)* The kindling flame has come—
Come as warmth and light and breath of God—
Come as power and love!

*(Congregational Hymn, unannounced, with words printed in bulletin. Speaker or minister may signal congregation to rise as organist or pianist begins introduction.)*

## SEE HOW GREAT A FLAME ASPIRES

Words: Charles Wesley     Hymn Tune: St. George's Windsor

("Come, Ye Thankful People, Come")

(1)

See how great a flame aspires,

kindled by a spark of grace.

Jesus' love the nations fires,

sets the kingdoms on a blaze.

To bring fire on earth he

   came.

kindled in some hearts it is;

O that all might catch the

   flame,

all partake the glorious bliss!

(2)

When he first the work begun,

small and feeble was his day;

Now the Word doth swiftly run,

now it wins its widening way;

more and more it spreads and

   grows,

ever mighty to prevail;

sin's strongholds it now

   o'erthrows,

shakes the trembling gates of hell.

(4)

Saw ye not the cloud arise,

little as a human hand?

Now it spreads along the skies,

hangs o'er all the thirsty land.

Lo! the promise of a shower

drops already from above;

but the Lord will shortly pour

all the spirit of [God's] love.

*(Speaker or minister seats the congregation. Speaker exits or sits.)*

## Part III: The Promise Is to You

**SOLO:**      And you shall be my witnesses to the ends of the earth,
For the promise is to you, and to your children,
And to all that are far off,
Everyone whom the Lord our God calls.

**UNISON:**   For the promise is to you—here in your homes,
Where husband and wife go different ways *(ADAM and EVE
enter from separate sides of the sanctuary.)*

40

And live in separate worlds,
Until the wall between them is so high
They can no longer see each other.

*(They speak from the sides of the sanctuary with their backs to each other.)*

**EVE:** How much time does he think *I* have? I work too, as well as helping with scouts, serving at the church, volunteering at school.

**ADAM:** Why doesn't she stay home once in a while?

**EVE:** All he wants to do is watch television.

**ADAM:** She doesn't understand the pressures I'm under.

**UNISON:** Separate worlds—walls that divide.

**EVE:** *(in anguish)* Adam, Adam, where are you?

**UNISON:** *(echo)* Where are you, are you, are you? *(pause)*
O Holy Spirit, come—come as holy fire.
Burn down the walls that they might step across into each other's worlds. *(They turn and move toward each other.)*
And talk and share and walk together
Toward the common goal of fellowship with God.
*(They walk to altar and stand facing it.)*

**SOLO:** And the promise is to you and your children—
Here in your homes—

**DARK:** Where parents command,

**LIGHT:** And children rebel,

**LIGHT AND DARK:** And each insists the other does not understand,

**UNISON:** Until the gap between them is so great
They can no longer even shout across it.

**EVE:** *(turning to ADAM at altar)* Please, Adam, talk to him. I can't make him understand. *(SON enters.)*

**ADAM:** Now you listen to me, Son. You've got to quit fighting with your brother. Don't you know it's wrong to fight?

**SON:** That's a switch. *You* don't think it's wrong to fight in a war. *(sarcastically)* And doesn't your religion say we're *all* brothers?

**EVE:** *(pleading)* And Son, you've just got to study more.

**SON:** What's the point of school? There's no future. We're gonna blow ourselves up or all die of *AIDS*.

| | |
|---|---|
| **ADAM:** | And running around with those no-good friends of yours has got to stop. They're all on pot or even worse. |
| **SON:** | My friends aren't bad; they just like to have fun. And smoking pot's no worse than you and your cocktails after work every night. |
| **ADAM:** | *(yelling)* That's enough! You heard me, and that's final. |
| **SON:** | Look! Weren't you ever young? You never understand. And I don't care. I'll do what I please. *(starts down aisle)* |
| **EVE:** | Stop him! He's headed for trouble. |
| **ADAM:** | *(starting after him)* Come back! Stop! Stop, I say! |
| **ADAM AND EVE:** | O God, he cannot hear us. |
| **SON:** | *(at back of sanctuary)* O God, they *will* not hear *me. (leaves; ADAM and EVE turn back to face the altar.)* |
| **UNISON:** | Come, Holy Spirit, come! With tongues of flame, leap out and bridge the gap That they may hear each other, And understand the yearnings each one has to speak And to be understood. *(pause)* |
| **SOLO:** | And the promise is to all that are far off— The world in which we live. |
| **MEDIUM:** | Where race and creed and social class blind us So we cannot see that God is Creator And all humankind related. |
| **SOLO:** | He is not really one of us—he's _____ *(black, white, Asian, gay, etc.)* |
| **SOLO:** | He's not important enough to be our leader. |
| **UNISON:** | *(gasp)* You cannot be one of us if you don't believe as we do. |
| **SOLO:** | *(shouting)* Spirit of light— |
| **LIGHT:** | Break in upon our hearts, So we may see within the night race and class and creed That all are children of thee. |
| **ADAM:** | *(turning from altar to face congregation)* And God, look here— where we hang signs upon one another, |
| **UNISON:** | Signs so wide and tall and thick we cannot see That back of them stand human beings just like ourselves. |
| | *(Next six lines are shouted fast and vehemently at one another.)* |

| | |
|---|---|
| **LIGHT:** | Conservative! |
| **DARK:** | Liberal! |
| **MEDIUM:** | Peacenik! |
| **DARK:** | Warmonger! |
| **LIGHT:** | Capitalist! |
| **DARK:** | Communist! |
| **SOLO:** | Spirit of Love— |
| **MEDIUM:** | Enfold us in thy warmth until we glow with fire<br>To melt the signs that hide our fellow human beings<br>And see them standing there, like us, in need of thee. |
| **WIFE:** | *(turning from altar to face congregation)*<br><br>And God, look here—<br>Where those with different views line up in separate camps<br>And shout demands, but cannot find the words to make the other understand.<br><br>*(The FOUR YOUTHS in modern dress and SON come down aisle, shouting).*<br><br>No nukes! No nukes! Ban the bomb! No more testing!<br><br>*(They join ADAM and EVE in chancel.)* |
| **UNISON:** | *(trying to out-shout the youth)* Law and Order! Law and Order! Law and Order! |
| **SOLO:** | *(breaking in)* SPIRIT OF POWER— |
| **DARK:** | Send thy tongues of flame to touch our hearts and lips,<br>And give us words that may be understood by all. |
| **CHANCEL GROUP:** | *(Point to congregation)* And the promise is to you—<br>Whom the Lord our God calls—here in this church, |
| **DARK:** | Not a building— |
| **LIGHT:** | Not a club— |
| **UNISON:** | But a people called by God<br>To be God's witnesses to the ends of the earth! |
| **CHANCEL GROUP:** | For the Spirit of the Lord is upon *you,* |
| **UNISON:** | Because God has chosen you to preach Good News to the poor |
| **CHANCEL GROUP:** | To proclaim release to the captives |

**UNISON:**     To open the eyes of the blind

**CHANCEL**
**GROUP:**      To set at liberty those who are oppressed.

**CHANCEL GROUP AND VERSE CHOIR TOGETHER:**

God has chosen you to witness that God is Lord of your life—not next year—not next month—but NOW!

Benediction by Minister: Go forth now with God into the world, which God created and loves.
Tell the Good News that God is alive.
Help the blind to see.
Release those who are imprisoned by hate and greed.
And may the God of light and power and love be with you and give you courage and peace. Amen.

# POETRY AND RECITATIONS

## *An Easter Prayer*

I sing this happy prayer, Dear God,
For joy and Easter-time,
For birds that sing
And earth so fair,
for springtime beauty everywhere!

And I know why—for Jesus lives!
In all the world today
It's "waking time."
And glad hearts say,
"We thank You, God, for Easter Day!"

*—Arletta Christman Harvey*

## *Savior, Teach Me, Day by Day*

Savior, teach me, day by day,
love's sweet lesson to obey;
Sweeter lesson cannot be,
loving him who first loved me.

With a child-like heart of love,
At your bidding may I move;
Prompt to serve and follow thee,
Loving him who first loved me.

Teach me all your steps to trace,
Strong to follow in your grace,
Learning how to love from thee,
Loving him who first loved me.

Thus may I rejoice to show
That I feel the love I owe;
Singing, till your face I see,
Of his love who first loved me.

*—Jane E. Leeson, 1842*

## ONE SOLITARY LIFE

Here is a man who was born in an obscure village, the child of a peasant woman. He grew up in another obscure village.

He worked in a carpenter shop until he was thirty, and then for three years he was an itinerant preacher.

He never owned a home. He never had a family. He never went to college. He never traveled more than two hundred miles from the place he was born.

He never did one of the things that usually accompany greatness. He had no credentials but himself. He had nothing to do with this world except the naked power of his divine manhood.

While still a young man, the tide of public opinion turned against him. His friends ran away. One of them denied him.

He was turned over to his enemies. He went through a mockery of a trial. He was nailed upon a cross between two thieves. His executioners gambled for the only piece of property he had on earth while he was dying, and that was his coat.

When he was dead he was taken down and laid in a borrowed grave through the pity of a friend.

Nineteen wide centuries have come and gone, and today he is the centerpiece of the human race and the leader of the column of progress.

I am far within the mark when I say that all the armies that ever marched, and all the navies that ever were built, and all the parliaments that ever sat, and all the kings that ever reigned, put together, have not affected the life of man upon this earth as powerfully as has that one solitary life.

*—Anonymous*


## MY EASTER PRAYER

May you walk a little surer
    On the path that lies before,
May you see a little clearer
    May you trust a little more.
May you come a little closer
    To the Lord of Love Divine,
That your heart may sing for gladness,
    Is this Easter prayer of mine.

*—Anonymous*

## MY RISEN LORD

My risen Lord, I feel thy strong protection;
I see thee stand among the graves today;
I am the Way, the Life, the Resurrection,
      I hear thee say,
And all the burdens I have carried sadly
Grow light as blossoms on an April day;
My cross becomes a staff, I journey gladly
      This Easter day.

*—Anonymous*

## CALVARY AND EASTER

A song of sunshine through the rain,
   Of spring across the snow;
A balm to heal the hurts of pain,
   A peace surpassing woe.
Lift up your heads, ye sorrowing ones,
   And be ye glad of heart,
For Calvary and Easter Day
   Were just three days apart!

With shudder of despair and loss
   The world's deep heart is wrung,
As, lifted high upon his cross,
   The Lord of Glory hung—
When rocks were rent, and ghostly forms
   Stole forth in street and mart;
But Calvary and Easter Day . . .
   Were just three days apart.

*—Susan Coolidge*

## AN EASTER PRAYER

God's blessing rest upon you
   This happy Easter Day,
God make His joy to shine
   As sunlight on your way;
God fill your heart with song
   So glad it will not cease;
God bless you every day
   With love and joy and peace.

*—Anonymous*

# BORROWED

They borrowed a bed to lay His head,
When Christ the Lord came down,
They borrowed an ass in the mountain pass
For Him to ride to town.
   But the crown that He wore
   And the cross that He bore
     Were His own.

He borrowed the bread when the crowd He fed
On the grassy mountain side;
He borrowed the dish of broken fish
With which He satisfied.
   But the crown that He wore
   And the cross that He bore
     Were His own.

He borrowed the ship in which to sit
To teach the multitude,
He borrowed the nest in which to rest,
He had never a home as rude,
   But the crown that He wore
   And the cross that He bore
     Were His own.

He borrowed a room on the way to the tomb,
The passover lamb to eat.
They borrowed a cave, for Him a grave,
They borrowed a winding sheet.
   But the crown that He wore
   And the cross that He bore
     Were His own.

The thorns on His head were worn in my stead,
For me the Saviour died;
For guilt of my sin the nails drove in
When Him they crucified.
   Though the crown that He wore
   And the cross that He bore
     Were His own,
They rightly were mine—instead.

*—Anonymous*